THE BULLET TRAIN

AND

OTHER LOADED POEMS

THE BULLET TRAIN

AND

OTHER LOADED POEMS

Ra Sh

10
Ten Glorious Years
HAWAKAL

Published by Hawakal Publishers, 185 Kali Temple Road, Nimta, Calcutta 700 049 (India)

First edition: April, 2019

Website www.hawakal.com
Email info@hawakal.com

Cover photo by Abul Kalam Azad | Front image from the series *Trap 1995* | Back image from the series *Crows 1985*. Cover designed by Bitan Chakraborty.

Printed and bound at S P Communications Pvt. Ltd. Calcutta 700 009

ISBN-13: 978-93-87883-57-4 (Paperback)

Price: INR 250 | USD 7.99

For
Rohith Vemula

Foreword

Here is cutting edge poetry at its sharpest and most unsparing. If poetry's primary task is to speak truth to power unmasking the horrid and the dark buried alike by the jingoist media and obscene sycophancy, these poems precisely accomplish that by the tactical deployment of black humor, stabbing sarcasm and mischievous word-play. They expose the pornography of majoritarian authoritarianism masquerading as triumphant democracy turning lynchers, abusers, rapists, murderers and arsonists into patriotic heroes, and human rights activists and truth-tellers into criminal traitors. Nothing escapes the poet's roving gaze: Kashmir's children blinded by pellets, small entrepreneurs impoverished by de-monetization, other minorities, peasants driven to suicide, the outcaste *dalits* and *adivasis* rendered homeless by corporate mining and deadly dams, the ribald parading of bullet trains and fighter planes while looters of public money sell diamonds in London and the poor small time beef peddler is lynched and little girls raped in front of dumb gods and deaf goddesses, all amidst sterile elite protests that end up seducing tourists. A true witness to the pornography of power politics in our cruel times.

K. Satchidanandan
March 21, 2019

CONTENTS

The Bullet Train

[The first *Aadhaar* linked poem in the world. By *Aadhar* No:
9876 5432 1001]

The Shinkensan Model accelerates to
217 miles an hour, cutting journey time
to 3 hours from Ahmedabad to Mumbai.
Mukesh sings *"Meri gaadi hai japaani"*
in a soulful studio radio.
Born post-war, Shinso Abe smiles
and waves and hugs like Hirohito.

This Bullet Train is the Brahmaasthra of the epics.
Or the Narayanasthra or the Rama Bana.
Sometimes, it is a Mohanasthra that drugs
billions of people putting them in a daze.

There is another Bullet Train.
A 7.65 Calibre Make in India model
that passes through stations with
strange names like Kalburgi South
Pansare West and Dhabolkar Central,
its destination set in Bangalore
where it rockets through a pulsating heart.

This train now will pass through
under skin arteries and veins and nerves
tunneling through bone marrow and muscles
till it comes to rest on a magnificent spine bridge,
perched like a toy train on a full moon night
till the slightest breeze causes the compartments
to topple into a depthless soul, one by one.

The Anthem

A black man sat in the Tagore theatre balcony
and an old man with a flowing white beard sat next to him
while the Anthem was being played.
The rest stood up.
These two remained seated.

The black man asked the bearded gentleman,
"Who da fuck're you, man?"

The saintly man said,
" I'm Tagore…and who art thou?"

The black man said,
" I'm Bob Marley and I stand up only for my rights."

The Valley of the Blind—A Crow Chronicle

a pellet is a precious pearl.
soft as a grain of rice.
kisses the eye like a lover.
caresses the pupil like your mom.

crows are vile birds, traitors,
who predict the arrival of armed guests
in riot gear and armored trucks.

crows in thirunaavaaya* perch on trees
and land on the rice balls offered
like long departed souls, ever hungry.
one of them is my dad.

(one day he vanished and came back weeks later.
he said he went visiting his crow brethren in
shreenagaram**.)

he said (my hindu dad said)
my hindu dad's hindu soul said:
"son, in shreenagaram, there's a crow for every man.
a platoon comes and people assemble.
all of them are blind, blinded, shot.
pellets doing henna designs
on their blank bloodied faces.
the gunners don't know where to shoot,
so they shoot the pellets at us crows
in the valley of the blind.
the ground is covered in crow quills.
crow beaks, crow wings, and crow blood

till hundreds of crows fly in from house tops,
perch on the guns and the masks and
peck at the malevolent eyes.

i flew away when the state began to bleed."

he dropped dead at the foot
of our mango tree.
he had no eyes.
my dad's soul was dead.

i removed 69 pellets from his heart
before cremating him.
i made a garland from the pellets
and gave it to my granddaughter to wear.

The Snow Girls

The battle lines were drawn up.
The snow girls with books in backpacks.
The olive green troopers with guns.

An eagle perched on a white cloud
relayed the proceedings to Times Now.

A snow leopard in distant mountains
stopped its hunt and waited.

Even a Yak in Tibet stopped its grazing
and looked towards the west.

A Bollywood film crew shooting a song
packed up and left.
The world grew still. The Dal lake grew still.
The waters in Jhelum paused.
In far away Kerala, people waited for the
channel debates to begin.

A hail of bullets mowed down the white harvest.
The olive green troopers advanced.
They saw.
Each girl who was felled held a red flower soaked in
blood.
And a handkerchief on which was embroidered,
With Love from Kashmir.

As if A...

As if a girl's scream fell on the deaf ears of gods, hills and
trees
As if a rape was not a rape, but just sticking pins into an inert
doll
As if a gypsy girl was not a girl, but a plaything of aspiring
ascetics
As if a temple was not an abode of God, but a rapist's
sanctorum
As if a girl was not a girl, but a body to crush, smash and
mutilate
As if a hole sprouted between her legs for the sport of
macho men
As if a law was not a law but a shredded page of history
As if a policeman was not a law protector, but a law breaker
As if a lawyer was not a lawman, but a law bender
As if a legislator was not a law maker but a law ender
As if a rape was an innocent act like plucking a flower
As if a land named Kashmir was not a heaven under the stars
As if a heaven named Kashmir was a hell open to rape
As if
As if
As if a girl named Asif...does not exist, didn't exist, will not
exist
As if Asif...was never raped, never tortured, never ravaged
As if Asif...is a myth, a fantasy, a lie, a fading photo
As if we are we were we will be....

Mr. Buff and Ms. Drug—a classified saga of love

Ms. Drug was a narcotic agent and a ninja in love
Mr. Buff was a vegan addicted to chewing grassy cud.
But, his majestic herd-watch on an elevated rail track
upturned wagon loads of counterfeit currencies
and map loads of coal, copper and gold mines
and *sudarshana chakra*s to saw down the trees.

Ms. Drug flew in to catch the mythical Mr. Buff and
spotted him on a wild hill with two suns on his horns.
Her clitoris throbbed at the sight of the night black figure,
but she engaged him in a war of weapons and narcotic
drugs.

Mr. Buff had never seen such a pretty thing
like a cotton cloud, fringes painted by a rainbow.
He locked her onto his horny horns and threw her on his
back
and enacted a dream like sequence of a Kurosawa war.

For nine days, their battle raged.
By day, they fought. By night, made love.
Washed each other's wounds.
Dressed them with herbal salves.
She sharpened his horns for him.
He honed her tridents for her.
Then, tired, they spent the night under the ogling spy
cameras.

Sleeping not a moment, attacking, withdrawing,
mounting, slipping, squeezing, releasing,

dreaming of endless days of war and nights of love.

Tenth day morn, a chopper landed
and chopped his head off her bosom.
She was dragged off as a drag queen
to Guantanamo as its first woman inmate
where all their progenies were aborted.
But, Mr. Buff resurfaced when the first bullion
rolled out from the Vedantic mine.

Mr. Buff was spotted on the denuded hill
with two suns on his battered horns.
Ms. Drug was piloting a captured chopper
in a daring escape to the East.

His nostrils had already caught her spoor.
He sauntered downhill to his people
to declare ninety nine years of war and love.

Love in the Time of Demonetization – I

took me four queues to notice her.
she took six.
am wearing the same shirt with scarlet leaves.
she, a *kalamkari* printed indigo *saree*.

in the eighth queue we stood body-trapped, back to front,
front to back.
she smelled my sperm, i, her ovum.
to the ninth queue we went together on her honda activa.
she got a pinky. i got none.

in the tenth, i got a pinky. she got none.
in the eleventh atm booth, we decided to make out.
she got in with me and i jammed the door.
we began to kiss and she began to strip.
the long queue anaconda shaped tried to swallow the glass
door heaven.

we did it slowly.
the slow lazy fuck.
the ones reserved for evenings of wine.
me leaning on the screen.
she leaning on me.
her butts did the slow gyrating dance.
pink flames played on her naked bum.

we screamed and the machine broke.
we fell through the chute to the innards of the reserve
bank

into a chamber where demonetized notes and freshly
printed currency
kept flowing in from chute after chute.

we rolled on the notes and went on rolling
notes plastered on our bodies
till the gdp, stock exchange, the government,
the army all crashed around us.

when we dragged ourselves out from the debris,
the parliament was a heap of rubble.
we waited in red cross street for the battered jeep
of Arnold Alois Schwarzenegger to pick us up.

Love in the Time of Demonetization – II

love budded in the second queue
as if it got a cue and arrow from cupid
as the shadows lengthened with the
wait for the cash.

at the fourth she
stood in front and i smelled her
sweat. at the counter i didn't see any
cash as she walked out with hers
her pink *dupatta* brushed my face
like in karan johar movies.

i followed
her pink self out, the machine cold
had run dry. in the next, i stood
before her and touched the warm
screen which came alive and showered
me with pink flowers. i let them
blow up in the air and as she walked
out cashless, the flowers rained on
her with pink bubbles filmi-like.

i thought we will meet in queue after
queue when she turned and asked me
where we could have coffee and
as things were settling down
like in dreams, she got a call -
there was cash in sbi in hauz khas
and i got a call there was cash in the
sib near regal and she rushed to

hauz khas and me to cp.

have been looking for her in queue
after queue but the queues died down.
and only the poor stood in queues and died.
pink *dupatta*s died too. and pink
bubbles no more.

we went cashless.
loveless. dream less. lifeless.
we swiped and swiped getting no love.

cupid's obituary on valentines day read
no arrows on flipkart.

The Strange Death of an Outcast

who was rohith vemula?
i knew many, not just the head without torso
that hung from a spider web.

a rohith vemula was my childhood pal
who saved me from the bite of a cobra.
he stepped on its head calling it a rat snake,
later died in the hospital sweating blood.

a rohith vemula saved me from drowning
when i was trying to pluck a lotus flower
in the local pond. he got sucked into the slush.

a rohith vemula pushed me to safety
when crossing a road. he got hit by the army truck.

a rohith vemula wrote my love letters for my beloved.
her family goons broke his limbs.

a rohith vemula sat with me in arrack shops, travelled
with me on long train journeys singing songs,
squatted with me on the fields sharing the same bottle to
wash up.

a rohith vemula taught me how to make a leaf spoon,
how to play *thalappanthu*,
how to angle with a hook and a worm.

a rohith vemula guided me through my adolescent
fantasies,
sold lottery tickets to me
seated on a makeshift wooden trolley,
paid 51 rupees for my wedding,
drove the three-wheeler which saved my child's life,

poured the first drops of black tea
into my just born granddaughter's thirsty mouth.

rohith vemulas crowd my life, criss crossing my life's
pathways as playmates, classmates, lovemates, workmates,
shaapmates.

so, who is this new rohith vemula
who hangs from a fine web of lies , conceit, loathing and
repulsion,
masterminded by an academic pool
where only vultures come to wash their beaks.

who is he to die so unceremoniously?
'like a dog,' 'like a dog,' my kafka wails
as someone slits his throat ear to ear.

72

This Day,
72 infants sounded the bugles.
72 infants hoisted the flag.
72 infants saluted the flag.
72 infants formed the infantry.
72 infants marched along the road.
72 infants crossed the Rapti.
72 infants ascended the Himalayas.
72 infants ascended Mount Kailas.
72 infants ascended the clouds.
72 infants entered the Milky Way.

Below, there was jubilation
on the birth of the blue God.
And the birth of a new nation.

How to Lynch a Man

it's really simple. what you need first is
a man, preferably alone, poor or looking
poor, carrying no weapons and exhausted
from work, starving, and apparently
belonging to a lower caste or is a muslim.

next you need a slogan. it could be anything
from *har har mahadev* to *jai durga* or
jai bajrang bali ki, or even a modern one
like *bharat chodo* or *go mata ki raksha karo*.

next you need a reason. this is the easiest
part, for reasons are aplenty and you just
need to pick one.

the lynching is a bit dicey for a beginner but
after one or two outings you become an expert.

hit his shoulders with a rod and his knees
with a log which will make him crumple
and show weepy eyes to the news channels.

let him have his moment of glory. then
keep on hitting his torso till he wriggles and
screams and then bring out the big knives.
this part the veterans will do—chop his body
at select places to put him out of action. when
he stops moving turn his body with two or
three kicks and unzip your *pyjama* and pee

26

into his mouth. he will still be breathing in the
pool of blood. now douse him with kerosene.
throw a light on him. step back to view your
fiery installation with the eye of an artist.

wait, he says something.
step closer to hear him say in burning agony
mother fuckers motherfuckers
burn in hell.

turn to the crowd and declare happily
look! he repented and shouted *vande mataram.*

Man with the Solar Brain

His brain awash with solar rays
the man with the solar brain
walks past the cotton fields
and the mobile towers
listening to the tweets and
the songs of extinct birds.

Extinct is he, a dead man walking,
but with solar winds
colliding with his body
packed in the barks of extinct trees.

He is the last man standing
in a field of dug up crops
and the rumble of a future city;
yet his pyre is yet to be lit
as he has his crematorium in the extinct sun.

Extinct corn, extinct buffalo,
extinct water, extinct air.
The extinct man with the solar brain
walks on bravely with a sun on his head.
The son of Solaris, the planet of dead green memories.

His phone rings, he picks up,
and from the phone flows out
that great evergreen Bollywood song
"Meri desh ki dharthi…"

Sweet Porn Soup

There was this pink cheeked girl
who served me Sweet Corn Soup
from a 'chinese' van at s.sarai
near the j.p. forest in dehli every night.

One day/night, she called me in the van
and taught me how to cook the soup.
The van smelt of chicken stock, spring onions,
fermented sauces, chillies, vinegar,
corn kernels, butter, garlic cloves,
carrots, beans, white pepper and corn flour.
Her nipples were little onions sautéed in butter.
Belly smeared with corn flour slurry.
Kernels popping in her sweet cunt.
She served herself hot to me and I
plastered her with red and green sauce
splashing vinegar behind her ears.

Throughout the night, we made
Love and dim sums
Love and chowmein
Love and spring rolls.

As it happens in art house movies,
the van was missing the next day
and the next and the next.

As it happens in badly written scripts,
the van was found on the banks of J'muna
near *antim nivas* in k.kunj.

On her bloated body, the witty rapists
had painted this with red sauce
"Sweet Porn Soup."

A Biblio Surgeon's Workbook

I am a book surgeon.
I took up bibliopathy when my dad,
who was a marxist book lover,
died of an unidentified illness.
I opened up his body to find
lenin's treatise 'left wing communism- an infantile
disorder'
in his right ventricle.

Since then I have visited many libraries
and treated many men and books.
Men who want to be books and books who want to be
men.

Some books need plastic surgery for a total make over.
I grafted bolano pages to indian poetry skins.
marquez to bengali cook books.
neruda to bhojpuri novels.
baudelaire to saral hindi translations.
shakespeare to panchatantram fables.
mao to amar chithra katha.
I saved many Indian marriages by inserting mast ram into
hanuman chalisa.

I am a darya ganj messaiah.

I am now in a high security press
(Where new 2000 rupee notes are getting printed)
with a secret mission to interpolate
Golwalker into Ambedkar.

Cross Border

Cross border is a corridor of death
dividing two houses.

There are two poets writing this cross border poem.
One from Nation A is slumbering
under a cross border tree under a cross border sun.
One from Nation B is also slumbering
under a cross border tree under a cross border sun.

Nation A poet wakes up, eats and catches a bus to town.
Nation B poet also wakes up, eats and catches a bus to town.
Nation A poet has a wife, two kids who go to school.
Nation B poet also has a wife, two kids who go to school.
Nation A poet's wife cooks, cleans, washes.
Nation B poet's wife cooks, cleans, washes.
Nation A poet reads Nation B poet's poems.
Nation B poet reads Nation A poet's poems.
Both poets love Madhubala.
Both poets love *sarson ka sag.*

Now, two soldiers stand between the two poets.
Neither enjoys the sun, neither enjoys the snow,
Neither likes flowers, neither has lovers,
Neither writes poems, neither reads poems,
Neither loves Madhubala, neither loves *sarson ka sag.*

When the poets return
Nation A soldier shoots Nation A poet.
Nation B soldier shoots Nation B poet.
Since both poets are dead, the poem ends here.

Post Rape Mortem

Today on the table lay a rainbow
twisted and maimed.
I dictated notes.
Death by mutilation after rape.

With a scalpel
I slit open the body color by color.

Violet ashened by shock
Indigo grafted on soiled blue
irreparably grilled by green
yellowed by a paste of orange peels
and red dust of a dead planet.

I signed the report.
"To determine the cause of death
the mortician needs more samples."

In the distance I heard the wail of rainbows.

Trisection

Now, the body had to be trisected.

Team A, Team B and Team C negotiated.
Negotiation was hush hush and in haste.
Team A wanted the thighs and legs.
Team B wanted the hands and breasts.
Team C wanted the torso and the butt.
Negotiations became heated.
Team A brandished sickles.
Team B unsheathed swords.
Team C flashed scimitars.

The body lay there wondering
why no one needed her head.
The head was pretty, curly hair,
merciful eyes, kind soft nose
and a mouth that always smiled.
Bright teeth and healthy gums.
and a fine functioning brain.
The head smiled at their arguments.

Finally, the warring factions
settled for an agreement.
Each got what they wanted.
Team A sawed off the legs thigh down
and stuffed them in a gunny bag.
Team B hacked off the hands and
sliced away the breasts, stuffing them
in a military issue rucksack.
Team C chopped off the head and

stuffed the torso, butt and all,
in a polished mahogany chest.

They made off in three directions
and the head was left alone on the grass.

Now, it began to sing a song
and some birds landed to listen.
Some animals too stood listening.
Soon, it became an orchestra
as the song of the chopped head
rose up and down rose up and down
like a leafy wave in the glade
till the forest became an ensemble
of clouds and pollen and flora and fauna.

And even some ancient stars that were long dead.

Appeal to the Great Teacher

You can teach me
How to burn alive a peacock
How to ride a truck over a peasant's thigh
How to pour molten tar into a man's mouth
Fire pellets into a kid's eyes.

You can teach me
How to hammer nails into a victim's palms
How to drive a pile into a woman's anus
Compose music from the screams of the helpless
Sing while quartering a convict.
You can even teach me
How to write poetry with the right hand
Flay someone's skin with the left
How to paint with a lynched man's blood
Chop in even slices a singer's tongue.

But, never never never never teach me
How to love.
Never never never never teach me how
To love.
You don't know
What I know.

Witch Burning at the Plaza

After the last witch was burned at the Plaza,
the rain god was so pleased and appeased that
he sent down a torrential rain to my thirsty city.

The witch was dead, but her flesh still smoldered
when the rain washed the ash down to the square.
The crowd who paid hefty sums in cash
to watch the spectacle, dispersed.
(The crowd always thins out after
the smoke hides the sex.)
The ash contractor's men swept up the ash with spades.

The eyes, breasts and womb of a witch remain unburned.
They are auctioned off at the site after the skull explodes.
This time, the bidding was fierce and competitive.
For, the witch who was burned was a famed poet.

A jeweler bought the eyes.
A purse-maker, the breasts.
Her lover bought her womb and
filled it with ink to dip a quill in.

Roland Garros

Match One
Serena rules the base line
Moving Kvitova like a chess piece
Till a drop shot in the fore court
Leaves her stranded
On the red clay court.
6-2, 6-4 the score reads.
The players shake out the red clay
from their Nike Air Max Mirabella 3 shoes.

Match Two
Maria grunts into another
Cross court shot
That makes Azarenka slide,
The ball just beyond her reach,
On the red clay court.
6-4, 7-6 the score reads.
The players shake out the red clay
from their Wilson Rush Pro Clay Lady shoes.

Match Three
Bouchard's ombre striped
Nike slam dress lifts in the wind
As she reaches high for the lob
From Radwanska's Babolat Lite racket
On the red clay court.
6-1, 6-3 the score reads.
The players shake out the red clay
from their Asics GEL-Solution Speed shoes.

End Game
Omega reads the time
At 20:00 GMT in Bastar.
The armoured vehicles move into
the village. Heckler & Koch MP 5 guns
spew bullets. Fleeing men shot with
Auto 9 mm 1A pistols. Huts burnt.
Women bludgeoned with rifle butts.
Dragged into MPVs. The blood of the shot
tribals running into the earth forming
a red clay ground.

20 men, 15 women the score reads.
The Cobras pick out the clotting blood
from their regulation boots.

Shakthiman

Not a superman or spiderman or batman
Am your local hero Shakthiman
But, folks, am not that manly hero
Only a pulicewala mare, now zero.

We are known in history
as moat jumpers for
Prathapji and Lakshmiji and
even mussalmans like that Tipu.
In *Vedic* times we were precious
stocks and shares like white cows.
Hundred horses for thousand cows
was the exchange rate then.

We went on decade long war expeditions
wrongly termed *ashwa medhams*.
While the cattle cowered in cow sheds
we died for men in battle fields.

Modern machines were measured by our power.
Yet, we got a raw deal folks, fed on horse gram and rum.
The cunning cows ran away with the cream.

Many fierce battles have we fought
for the venerable Indian police
as mounts for lathi wielding skull-bashing
MC BC spewing, betel-chewing cavalrymen.
against suspicious looking anti-national men.
But, alas, this time the cunning cows did me in.

Am a wax doll now with a meager pension
an artificial leg which hardly holds my weight.
A mere mare I am and the
cowman knew it for sure.
If a stallion, I would have
deflowered his arse.

Making Chai in Jahan Pannah

The fifth day of my research
Barakhamba Feroze Shah Akbar Aurobindo
I stopped by the small chai stall
of the blind old woman for ginger tea.

"Tej patthi" I said and looked around.
" Where's your daughter?" She pointed
At the Jahan Pannah forest. A nourishing
smile lighting up her 90-year-old face.
"Making pottery there."

I entered the forest to find it so calm.
Shah Pur Jat Panch sheel Hauz Rani
She was making pottery between
two large rocks. I took out my mobile.

"I spin the wheel of poetry not potty."
"Acha, tho, banale chai."

Two deer came close smelling fresh nilgiri chai.
The world spun boiled red in her kettle.

It was an excellent brew.
It was an excellent poem.

Next morning, I found her making pottery
on Raisina Hill between North and South Blocks.

The red tea flowed along Raj Path
and licked the flame at India Gate.

Then, Abida Parveen started her *riyaz* on Vijay Chowk.

I collapsed among the cosmic bodies when she suppliantly
sang
"Yeh sab tumhara karam hai Aqaaaa."

I woke up between the thighs of Kunti
in Silent Valley with my hands probing
the breasts of Diti and Aditi, but Abida kept
singing "*So jaa, puttar*, you aren't ready yet."

I forgot to sound the clarion for
the war of the blue violet blue flowers.
A bull dozer had crushed their petals.

A Tale of Two Cities

Hauz Rani and House Raja were sibling cities.
They had binary vision on everything.

When Tendulkar hit Shoib into the stands
Hauz Rani wore a deathly silence.
When Inzamam hit successive sixers off Kumble
House Raja ground its teeth.

While Hauz Rani ate buffalo meat
House Raja had *bhindi* and *tinde*.
While Hauz Ràni had a row of kebab stalls
House Raja shops sold *jalebi* and *rasmalai*.

All hell broke loose when a House Raja boy
fell in love with a Hauz Rani girl.

A few got killed, a few raped, a few shops burned.

Geographically, Hauz Rani stood no chance
as a battalion of House Raja police encircled it.

The House Raja boy is now an IT guy in Massachusetts
while the Hauz Rani girl is grazing goats in Syria.
But, in reality, both were burnt and mixed in a concrete
mixer
and poured into two separate pillars
of the spanking new mall coming up where Hauz Rani
once stood.

But, then, who is the couple I met in Pondi
selling delicious kebabs like hot cakes?
When I said I was from Dilli, he served me some hot
*jalebi*s too.

Then, their daughter ran in from school
and I asked her name.
She shyly lisped, "Hauz Rani."

Execution of a Woman during the Reign of Akbar, the Great!

Anarkali was walled alive
while the constipated Emperor watched.

Her pink-assed lover was far away
biting naked women in between battles.

Anarkali thought, "This old creep
had cobbled up a religion
plagiarizing heavily from two religions.
Yet, he is here, hooked on his weed,
supervising the death of a woman!
What am I to him? A roach? An insect?
Look at him coming towards me
to adjust a brick here, the mortar there.
What a guy, man! What a lousy guy!
What kind of a prick is this great man!
Are all men pricks? Even Salim?"

Far away, the third woman was sucking
Salim's prick desperately
trying to raise it at least a nanometer.

Anarkali saw it all and broke into laughter
full of merriment and amusement.
"If only I could move a limb, I could have
danced a last tango in Dilli with that mason boy!"

Her laughter woke up the drooling old man.
He barked out orders and the masons
doubled their speed to seal up the wall.

Anarkali laughed for a long time
long after her immurement.
She was still laughing 400 years later
when archaeologists broke open the wall.
Her standing grave guarded by a female serpent.

The Arithmetic of Protest

766 is a magic number, said the Greeks.
When you near this number all earlier numbers
shed their wrappings and dance like flames.

On a blackboard in Statue junction, I write this number
and calculate many permutations.
The pairs of feet that passed him by in a second
equals 2 x 60x 60x24x 766 = 13,23,64,800, say 13 crores.
The 2011 census pegs the population of Kerala at 3.33
crores.
Which shows that Kerala trampled all over him
four times in 766 days,
without seeing him.
That's statistics for you.

I dig for more interesting data like
The number of idlis consumed in Ananda Bhawan for 766
days,
The number of beers guzzled in Hotel Pankaj in 766 days,
The number of coconuts burst in the Ganapati temple in
766 days,
The number of books bought in DC or Modern Book
House in 766 days,
The number of makeshift hearths lighted for two
Pongalas,
The number of activists in the political rallies that end
there,
The number of delegates who attended two IFFKs,
The number of connoisseurs at the cultural evenings in
VJT Hall,

The number of people, who attended weddings in Sree
Moolam Club,
The number of buses, cars, autos, bikes, scooters,
cacophony
That passed him by for 766 days,
without seeing him.

When a man is alone, he turns invisible.
So said Thiruvalluvar or someone or no one.

The Gift

You should be on an islet.
Surrounded by a coral red sea.
With three blue coconut trees.
An ochre cave.
A copper cat and a silver dog.
Green rabbits in deep holes.
Yellow mice and indigo snakes.
A chromium lake of fresh water.
A dozen olive brown fruit laden trees.
A blood crescent in the sky.

No courts, no cameras,
No hooligans, no policemen.
No Governments, no states.

You are a gift.
Wrapped. Untouched.
In an islet.

A magnetic storm lashes.
A galactic lightning strikes.
A diluvial rain screams.

The islet dissolves
Sand by sand
In each rainstorm.
The sea sucks you in.
The whales ferry you to the deep sea bed.
Where a million iridescent flowers bloom
To welcome you and call out to you
"Hadiya!"

Protest Tourism

They stood for a day.
They stood for a week.
They stood for a month.
They stood for a year.
They stood for a decade.
They stood for a century.
They stood for a millennium.
They are still standing.

Meanwhile, the ground on which they stood changed to an
express highway, a football stadium, a performing arts
centre, a hospital, an army camp, a water theme park and a
graveyard.

Now, it is a dead volcano
with a placid blue lake in the crater
that attracts one million tourists per year.

Onam—setting the record straight

[translation of a poem by Sahodaran Ayyappan]

At the time of Maveli's reign
All men got treated the same.
A reign of joy. A reign sans mishaps.
No frauds around, no cheating ones.
Not even the smallest speck of a lie.
No untouchables, no pollution,
No degradation. No such perverse ways.
No animal sacrifice. No *poojas* with offerings.
No agent between man and divinity.
No rude and senseless gods.
No rich and no poor.
No dearth of capital.
Men producing wealth for all
By toiling hard as each was able.
Learning the letters without a hitch.

At the time of Maveli's reign,
Men and women had equal freedom.
Men were civilized at their own will.

The ruling Brahmins grew wary of this.
Invited the sly dwarf Vamana home.
Who donned the role of a mendicant!
By guile he ensured Maveli's fall.
Dispatched him to the underworld.

The four-caste system came to be.
Turning earth into living hell.
They began to say men polluted men.

Evil untouchability began its reign.
Overpowered the weaker ones.
Licked the feet of the powerful ones.
Drank the sweat of the poorer folk.
While the lazy ones grew in girth.

If the poor happened to utter the alphabets,
Their tongues were put to the sword.
Women became dolls to play with.

How many centuries have we been
Bearing this yoke in silence?
Brothers, for us to rise again
Better rouse up our fellow brothers.

Listen!
The Brahmin religion is a rotten one.
One that crushes the ones who follow.
Religions create divide amongst us.
Discard religions once and for all.
Truth and Virtue are the pure religions
To guide us on to a noble living.
A religion ordained by the Great ones past.

Discard Vamana's morals, we must.
Bring back Maveli's reign, we must.

Notes to the Poems

The Bullet Train

In memory of Gowri Lankesh, Journalist, who was shot dead. Also, Kalburgi, Pansare, Dhabolkar, and other rationalists, who were shot dead in the same manner.

The Anthem

Written during IFFK—International Film Festival of Kerala 2016, when a Supreme Court ruling ordered the National Anthem be played in cinema halls before each show when everyone had to stand up in respect. Tagore is the poet who wrote the Anthem. Reggae singer Bob Marley is famous for his song Get up Stand up; Stand up for your rights.

The Valley of the Blind—a crow chronicle

Written after the Indian soldiers started using pellet guns against agitating locals in Kashmir.
Tirunaavaya – a water front where Hindus do offerings to departed souls.
Shreenagaram – Srinagar

The Snow Girls

This battle is entirely imaginary and has no resemblance to any event anywhere on this globe.

As if a…

An 8 year old nomadic Gujjar Muslim girl was abducted and confined in a temple in Jammu for more than a week and continuously raped by a gang of men before being killed. It took 4 months for a charge sheet to be filed. Lawyers in Jammu were protesting against the arrest of the culprits instead of following the law.

Mr. Buff and Ms. Drug—a classified saga of love

Written as a reaction to the Government taking over aboriginal lands for mineral mining by companies such as Vedanta.

Love in the Time of Demonetization – I

Written after the Demonetization of 500 and 1000 rupee notes by the Indian Government in Nov 2016. Since 86% of the cash in circulation was withdrawn, lives went into a dizzy. Long queues waited for cash in ATM booths. Small businesses collapsed. In cities, people rushed from ATM to ATM in search of cash. 'Pinky' refers to the new pink 2000 Rupee notes printed by the Government.

Love in the Time of Demonetization – II

Written after the Demonetization of 500 and 1000-rupee notes by the Indian Government.

The Strange Death of an Outcast

Rohith Vemula was an active *Dalit* youth engaged in a protracted skirmish with the administration of the Central University, Hyderabad, who hanged himself to death in his hostel room. His death raised protests in Universities all over India.

72

Written after 72 infants died in a hospital for want of oxygen in the Gorakhpur constituency of the present UP Chief Minister. Predictably, the ruling party lost here in the next bye election.

How to Lynch a Man

Many lynchings took place in the northern belt of India against Muslims in the name of alleged cow slaughter and beef trade.

Man with the Solar Brain

Written after a huge farmers' rally that almost overran the city of Mumbai a few years back. A farmer on the march was spotted carrying solar batteries on his head.

Sweet Porn Soup

Related to no particular incident or related to all such incidents of rape and murder of women.

A Biblio Surgeon's Workbook

A poem about the art of rewriting history that right wing fascists indulge in.

Cross Border

A poetic view of two nations in conflict.

Post Rape Mortem

Written after the molestation of many transgender and queer people in Kerala.

Trisection

About gender violence.

Appeal to the Great Teacher

About freedom of expression.

Witch Hunting at the Plaza

About gender violence.

Roland Garros

A parallel study of the accessories of sports and the accessories used in the annihilation of tribals in India. The US produces the best sportswear and also exports maximum arms and ammunition to the world.

Shakthiman

A Hindutva party MLA broke the legs of a fine police horse which died later.

Making Chai in Jahan Pannah

A poetic journey between some eras placed on location in the geography of present day Delhi. Such old tea makers can be seen on the streets of modern day Delhi. Jahan Pannah is a forest area slowly being encroached upon. Once such forest areas are completely removed, Delhi will gasp for fresh air. Already it is one of the most polluted cities of the world. Raisina Hill is where the President's residence stands now. A bee line runs from it between the North and South Head Quarters of the Central Government, running up to India Gate, a mausoleum for Indian soldiers who died for the British during the First World War. Vijay Path is that road down which the Republic Day Parade takes place. Vijay Chowk is a large square on the road from which Vijay Path starts. Abida Parveen is a Pakistani Sufi singer. Kunti is the mother of Pandavas and also the name of a river in Kerala on which stands the Silent Valley National Park. Diiti and Aditi are the primordial mothers from whom all life began.

A Tale of Two Cities

Hauz Rani is a small Muslim village in south Dilli almost entirely encircled by a place named Malaviya Nagar which consists mostly of Hindu refugees from Pakistan and is a Hindutva Party bastion. We, some Mallus and Bengalis, used to regularly go to Hauz Rani to enjoy gost or keema or half biriyani along with the largest breads I have seen.

Execution of a Woman during the Reign of Akbar, the Great!

Akbar, the Great, had a son name Salim who later became known as Emperor Jehangir. He fell in love with a court maid named Anarkali. Infuriated Akbar, who had started a new syncretic religion called Din-I Ilahi, killed her by burying her alive within a wall.

The Arithmetic of Protest

A 25 year old man lay on the sidewalk in front of the Kerala Secretariat for 766 days, demanding justice for his brother who was beaten to death in police custody in a Trivandrum police station. It took 'progressive' Kerala 766 days to see him lying there on the sidewalk.

The Gift

The Hadiya case in which a Hindu girl converting to Islam and marrying a Muslim man became a topic of much discussion in Kerala. I am one of those who believe that the Hadiya case exposed the Kerala society for what it really is now. The many arms of the State apparatus (including the courts, the police, the political parties in power, the media etc) were brutally used to crush individual spirit and freedom. And, we turned spectators. But, luckily for the couple, the Supreme Court set aside all arguments against them. The word 'Hadiya' means 'Gift.'

Protest Tourism

Tribals of Kerala went into a 'standing' protest outside the Head Quarters of the Kerala Government. They merely stood there for ages. They didn't know that Kerala was slowly transforming into a tourism society.

Onam—setting the record straight

A translated poem on Onam, a festival of Kerala, which describes the just rule of King Mahabali (Maveli) till the Four caste system was heralded by Vamana, the Brahmin. An old folk song re-rendered by early 20th Century social reformer Sahodaran Ayyappan.

Ra Sh (Ravi Shanker N) has published several English-language poems in many national and international online and print magazines. His poems have been translated into German and French. *Architecture of Flesh* is his sole collection, the second edition of which came out in Oct 2018. He is an established translator and critic.

www.ingramcontent.com/pod-product-compliance
Lightning Source LLC
Chambersburg PA
CBHW021145020426

42331CB00005B/907